Girls Grow Up

Girls Grow Up

creative direction + poetry:
Christie Maragos

drawings + whimsy:
Julia Monson

EVERY GIRL'S DIARY...

is equal parts wishes
and confessions.

Some, which never see
the light of day:

too potent for
their mother's ears,
too worrying for their friends.

The thrills and pain
we keep to ourselves,
buried in the sand.

EVERY GIRL'S DIARY...

is equal parts romance and regret,
happiness and shame:

a written testament on how love
can transform us if it's pure
and ruin us if it's not real.

Read our words only if you want
to be forever changed and
a witness to our truth:

"how girls grow up a million ways"
but our hearts remain the same:

PURE AND BRAVE.

FOR ME

contents

virgin / nymph

How easily I changed
from a virgin to a nymph
under your direction.

Butterfly squeezed out
of chrysalis with
your discretion.

I USED TO WONDER

I used to wonder how a girl
could ever leave you
(with that tongue ring
like a star in your mouth).

Making dreams I didn't
even know I had come true.

You had the smile of someone
who knows everything
before it happens.

I was a good girl unraveling
—a testament to how desire
is a spell when you haven't
felt it before.

The next morning:
your grandmother asks you
why angels were chanting
in your bedroom,
why you left the window
open during a storm.

When I begged you
to show me my own body,
your touch a better teacher
than my own.

REAP AND SOW

You make me orgasm
in a soccer field,
sunlight coating my
solar plexus.
Blades of grass form
a blanket beneath us.

It feels like earth
is giving me a hug.

I am your muse
that entire summer
and I wonder
who taught your hands
what they know,
how to reap and sow.

THIS WAY

Euphoria makes us blind
to all reason,
a dream girl's form of escapism.

When they asked me
to pick my poison:

I chose you.

You fall in love with the
consistency
of my self-abandon,

the ease of my submission,
but never with the truth:

I am only this way with you.

THAT WAY

You want my heart
but you keep yours locked.

You bury the key
in every new woman
who touches you—*foreign*

to the ways you've done
this before and promised
it was the real thing.

You are always on the search
for a woman whose love
will end your self-hate.

Tell me when you find out
that love doesn't work that way.

GIRL NEXT DOOR

Girl next door
you stalked on Instagram.
The perfect combination of
slutty & sweet like a sour key.
You make me into a metaphor
for all your friends.
You save me in your phone
with the princess emoji.
But touching my body is
an obstacle course of consent
and insomnia means I can't always
sleep in the same bed with you.

Girl next door
you cherished with
the resigned ease in which
we commit to something
we want—only to discover
it's a different thing entirely.
You were in too deep to
abandon the initial fantasy.
The way it felt to hold it
close to your heart
like it was the *real* me.

DRIVE-IN

The first time we met
you undressed me at the drive-in.
The one with the old swing set I liked
because its wide-set frame let you
feel like you were swinging
directly into the sky.

We kissed in the backseat
when it got dark enough to hide
our intentions and you pled
between caresses,
and heavy breathing,
and foggy windows,
but I didn't let you
"go down" on me.

I wasn't ready to give you
that power.

I didn't want to admit
that the only orgasms I'd had
up until now had been with
the gentle reassurance
of my own hands,
the safety of them.

Because men always touched me
too rough (the way porn taught them)
with hands they forgot to wash.

Fingernails full of dirt
from helping their dad with
construction work in the summer.

Leftover lust on their hands
from ex-girlfriends who clung to
them like the adhesive on an envelope.

Men always touched me
like my body didn't matter,
like it was an extension
of everyone else they've known,
like I was a placeholder for the affection
that was never returned to them
from their high school crushes,
or the heartache that never left them
from the women they tried to love
but failed somehow.

I always had to escape from these men
because they brought me to places
I never wanted to see.

They told me my skin was a dead end.

They acted like my heart was
a grave not worth visiting.

But you were different.

You brought flowers to all my old selves.
You sat in the grass with me telling stories
about sunsets that fall into our lap,
and kisses that stop time,
and dreams that reveal more
than what we want to know.

You wanted to see every part of me:
every truth come to light,
every stone of my past turned over,
"who I am" vs. what is just
a coping mechanism
for what I've gone through.

You wanted the pain I tried so hard
to keep buried, but sometimes
fear is all we know and letting
someone else be a part of it
doesn't feel safe *either.*

LESS
a poem about coercion

It's always, "just a little bit."

(in your car)
(in your car)

I'm always just a little bit, *less.*

—I feel like a teenager again when men touch me despite my refusal. It's like there are tissues inside their ears.

CHAMELEON

You learn quickly
that I am always changing,
chameleon in a hot girl's body.

You call me a 24/7 tease,
like my body is a drive-through
open late.

Like my pussy is a neon
welcome sign for when men
get lost in their own hedonism.

SEX

We have sex every time we see each other
—the predictable chemistry of two
damaged people who want love
(but built walls the first time
it departed).

I make several, sometimes futile
attempts to get to know you:
the things you work hard for,
your dream life and its
anchor points,
the women who made roots
and then left you on read.

Your intimacy routine is taking
a shot of tequila before taking
your clothes off,
like there's a predisposition to hurt
you are trying to numb.

My intimacy routine is feigning
shyness so you tell me
I am beautiful,
so you touch me like
you are putting me
back together,
so you take your time with me.

CAT AND MOUSE

Like cat and mouse,
you expect me to chase you.

You are used to women
offering themselves up like
the wrapped candies they give
when you leave a nice restaurant.

I am used to men who act feverish
in their attempts to pursue me
like my hair on their pillow
is a chance at salvation.

There is already a disconnect between us.
We've grown selfish in our habits.
Neither of us will compromise.

Why should I chase you?

When love comes so often,
begging for me to notice it.

SILVER LINING

(1) My desires have a life of their own:

a glass half-full that eventually
spills over—

because you keep adding more to it.

(2) It's like I am collecting heartache
in third date promises.

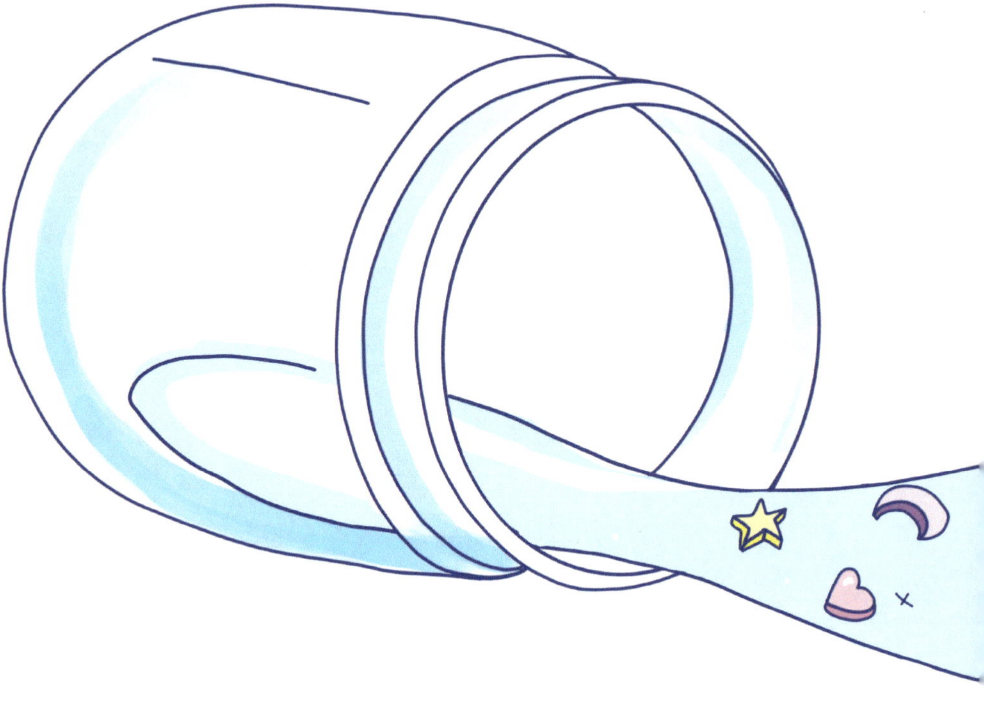

(3) But I can't stop finding
the silver lining
in passion that disarms me.

(4) How it reminds me:

"I am human"

and at the mercy of *everything.*

SNOWFLAKES

You think “new” love will resurrect you

so you open your mouth to it.

You try to catch snowflakes

on your tongue,

sucking him *off.*

HOLD THE MAP

I succumb to desire even though it has taught me
that men leave as quickly as they make promises:

heart in the wrong place / head in the clouds
when they touch me.

My body / just a city to mark on a map
with a red thumbtack / tell people they saw it
first-hand / a safe place for men

who are refugees from their own past.

My body is comic relief after a lifetime
of never finding home / but my body is
deserving of real love:

not just hungry touches / not just promises
made in passion's haste.

But you lure me close using my own heart as bait.

You curate versions of the person you'll never be,
so I can't find holes in the person you are

and in having this faith that you are better than
the men I've known / I become just another
body to weed through. Vulnerable.

Like plucking every petal off a flower and
discarding its stem / women are just

a game for you.

And ironically, women like us who are dying
to be loved in a way that doesn't *degrade* us—

we think the men who can't really see us
can be convinced to take a second look.

We imagine that if we laid ourselves out
piece by piece / they would finally see our value.

We try to impress these men with a past that
doesn't sound like we barely came out alive:

a watered-down version of our truth
that they can digest
and still find us desirable.

But the less they see our worth,
the more we doubt it too.

We live our lives looking for proof
that we are lovable because history
tells us that we just miss the mark
of something worth cherishing.

But I'm not ashamed for having a heart
so open to love / I leapt when I should
have approached with caution / I trusted
when I should have asked questions.

I'm not ashamed for having a heart that looks
for silver livings because it is a testament
to how I always see the good in people
when sometimes there is none.

I recognize that not everyone deserves my body
and the heart it protects. Not everyone deserves
to hold the map / to visit / *to stay.*

AFFIRMATION

1

Men who don't know what they want
expect me to tell them.
My body a fortune to unravel
and shove in spare pockets.
The sentiment of me worth keeping
(if only) to look at again by accident.

I am a memory bank for lust.
The affirmations I recycled from
the women I look up to *don't* work.
But their unfabled confidence
inspires me to try harder,
to fit the self-love mould.

2

It takes 21 days to form a habit.
I assume this applies
to a school of thought too.
I want these women who have
never been shined by hurt
to explain how,
I have told myself I am beautiful
my whole life in every mirror
but it never sticks.

COMPLICATED

I have a complicated relationship with my face.

My face lacks the basic symmetry I have come
to appreciate in other faces.

Girls who can be transformed
so easily by makeup and a nice haircut
inspire deep envy I cannot shake.

They say:

your face is the face of someone
you loved the most in your past life.

How healing to believe this.

SAFETY CHAIN

"I miss the things
we used to do together."
The guy I lost my virginity
to messages me during mercury
retrograde (and suddenly, I am brought
back to deepthroating him in a hot car—
my hair sticking to my forehead in protest) and
every experience which felt like a low point in my life
is amplified when I read those words because they
remind me of what I've learned since watching
the movie *Thirteen*: that men will reduce our
entire beings to a moment of bad girl ecstasy
and it's ironic that I too can only remember
him in parts: the overflowing fruit bowl in
his kitchen which always appeared
untouched, the ten cardboard
air fresheners in his car in
Black Ice scent.

He fulfilled the cliché of every guy
I wish I never met but went to bed with
and I heeded the warnings of my
overprotective mother when she said,

"Men will come around and they will *hurt* you."

I was dutifully naïve to this—as though my own
good intentions could change theirs, as though
my own open heart could prove her wrong.

But I am tired of looking for the good apple
in a bunch of rotten ones.

And maybe that's why my mother gave up on love
because she knows how men have a tendency
of flocking back home to a woman's body
to be baptized again.

But my body was built for a better purpose
than to console the hearts of men who
put me on a pedestal and still left.

Because nothing can stop my body
from becoming my own haven.

A truth so valuable it warrants a safety chain.

This is what girls should be taught
but instead we are taught
to protect a man's ego,
to forgive malice disguised as love.

I often think about a girl I used to call my best friend,
how it was almost ceremonious the way we met
and made roots so quickly:

equally bewildered by the men in our life
who said one thing but meant another.

I admired this girl for her relentless pursuit of love
but she had the wrong idea about it from the start.
She chased after the men who made it clear
they didn't want her.

She put all of her efforts into transforming
their perception as though she could determine
the value they had adhered to her
before they even touched her.

She thought they could be convinced
by her beauty if she was in the right light.
She forgot her mind like it's not the
most valuable thing in her possession.

Why are girls still taught to be nice to men
who know *nothing* about softness?

Our bodies treated like:

a wound that reopens
a shop that never closes
a national holiday

My first boyfriend called my cellphone
47 times asking for a second chance
and 15-year-old me was painfully naïve
and thought his desperation meant he loved me
and this became a pattern in my life:
forgiving careless men, trying to heal them

—but their healing is just not my responsibility.

How freeing to only go
where love flows and protects me.

To only kiss men who mirror
my own worth back to me.

SUSPENSE

The men I end up wanting the most
are the ones who refuse
to open their heart,
who keep me in suspense for it.

Because the less they give,
the more they keep their power.
A heart like his must be rare if
he never shows it to anyone.

I imagine a gold mine in his chest
but when I lay my head there,
it's like knocking a fruit and
hearing the hollow.

The thrill of the chase loses its thrill,
the same way flowers wilt and force us
to discard them. Men like that are
stepping stones best avoided.

Your destiny will always be:

a love that doesn't ask you to
lose yourself just to have it.

CAUTION TAPE

I spent a decade losing my virginity
to a different set of hands,
convinced that I would
find love this way.

But undressing for a stranger,
no matter how earnest a pursuit,
is pleasure wrapped in caution tape.

SOUL SEARCH

It is easy to assume he is a dream come true
when you don't know what your dreams are.

—keep looking

A MAN LIKE YOU

I don't want to end up with a man
like you / I am too full

my grandmother says
I light up a room

she is forgetting but she
remembers to tell me this

I want to marry a man who sings
in the shower / who paints clouds
on my back with 2-in-1 shampoo

who makes fried eggs that are runny
but not raw / this takes practice

I want to marry a man who thinks
love is a 12-step program because

the first ten steps are being present
and the last two are asking God

I want to marry a man who thinks
intimacy is brushing teeth together*

who kisses me like he only has
one chance to get it right / who
tends to my body like it is the earth

if anything is rushed / nothing will grow

**inspired by Gabrielle Zevin*

ONCE GALAXIES

Women are beautiful,
worthy of velvet ropes
and museum walls.
Women are beautiful,
but men make us disposable.

I've seen women with fingers
that once cradled stars
have their wings clipped.
I've seen women who
were once galaxies
reduced to empty boxes
by men who don't know
the difference between
loving someone and
dimming them.

I promise I've outgrown the lust
of men who call my body *art*
but treat it like it's garbage.

I promise.
I promise.

The appeal of the past only exists
because I've become so familiar with it.

Trauma—an invisible friend
that follows you everywhere,
holds your hand and kisses your wrists.
But eventually, you can say no to it.

I have taken my clothes off
for too many predictable men
but no one has seen my soul.

And in this way of never
being truly vulnerable,
I've gained nothing from men
but the same scripted emptiness,
the same fear reflected back at me.

I've gained nothing but dead ends.

I don't want to keep operating
from a place of deep-rooted fear.
I don't want the chance that the past
will repeat itself to consume me.
But every time I have been soft,
I have been used.

I must keep myself at a distance
from people who make me feel
unsafe, unworthy, unlovable.

They don't see me the way I see myself.

Creative.

Resilient.

Kind.

Strong.

They don't see me at all.

old pain / new leaf

I want to build a white picket fence
around the girl who was still
learning her worth

because no one taught her
the right way to honour herself.

No one taught me that my body
could be a celebration just for me.

TWO WEEKS

1

Two weeks without a touch.
I reach for the vibrator I bought on a whim
and forgot about.
I position myself.
I press buttons in no particular order:

fast
slow
jumpy
fast, again.

It's stimulation (only calculated)
and I'm wholeheartedly convinced
that nothing in this world
compares to genuine passion.

2

A beautiful woman I barely know
(with full, heavy breasts and
hair like a Disney princess)
confides in me that she only
has sex every couple of years.

She counts off on her hands for me,
the months since a man
last touched her.

I *die* at the thought.

LONELY

I'm lonely—but not
lonely enough
to take you back.

Lonely in the practical way
of unripened fruit no one chooses
unless it's the only thing there.

I tell myself:

I am the one who should
be choosing me.

Let the years with you
wash off in the shower,
clog the sink like old hair.

We always view loss as a curse,
but sometimes holding on
is the only grief.

CHOOSE YOU
GIRL PWR
DON'T TEXT HIM

SOMETHING DIFFERENT

I have learned
that giving of oneself
will not feel like a sacrifice
if the person gives back,
and that waiting for
someone to change
is like picking all the fruit
from a tree and asking it to
grow something different.

THE TOWER
THE LOVERS

LOST CONNECTION

I call my ex to tell him about
a terrible day and we end up
having phone sex,
because comforting me
has never been his strong suit.

He *comes* and it's only a rustle
of a sheet on the phone
followed by a few seconds
of silence.

There is no goodnight kiss,
no recycled sentiments of

"I miss you,"
or

"Things could be different."

Just clarity that he saw
I was vulnerable and took
what he could from it.

GAG REFLEX

I used to test my gag reflex
with how many secrets I could swallow.
I used to carry every terrible thing
that had happened to people I loved,

a sacrificial lamb
can keep us alive
with its softness

thinking I could ease their burden
with my existence,

but softness
can only remain that way
if it is met with love.

All the things I didn't want to see
about myself have become
fossils inside my stomach.
Hard, lumpy truths.

But now that I'm awake
and realizing things
and feeling the feelings
I tried to extinguish,

I feel like I've fallen behind
in the grand plan for my life
and all I have to show for it
are past conquests and poetry.

I ASKED TIME

I asked time to stop
so I could memorize
your mouth making
promises it wouldn't keep,
so I could remember
the feeling of losing myself
for a love that wouldn't notice
I was barely treading water.
A love that wouldn't miss me
when I ran out of ways
to satisfy it.

I wanted to keep close
how you managed to
leave me empty when
I was full to begin with.
How you dimmed my light
just to count *stars-that-wouldn't*
give-you-their-wishes because
they knew how things came
easy for you. How it was never
a matter of "if you deserve me"
but—"how could you *have* me?"

STINGS

1

You forget how to take a shower alone:
my moan inside your ear.

My soapy kiss and expectant tongue
like a montage of what you lost.

You sleep on the edge of the bed
leaving room for my ghost to crawl in
to relive the past just once.

2

I suppose you feel my absence
now that you've made a place
for me—now that I've graduated
from being a secret.

I suppose it stings.

IMESSAGE:
I MISS YOU SO MUCH BABY

ABANDON

Almost everything
you abandon
will try to come back,
excuse in hand.

The irony in how
you wanted me most
when I never wanted to
see you again.

THE OLD ME

I don't recognize myself
and I'm glad because
I don't want to memorialize her.

She is sticks and stones
and boys who *hurt* you.

She is a curfew put in place
for your own good
that went ignored because
rebellion feels free during youth
(but you pay for it later).

She is intuition you didn't trust
because it warned you about the
people you loved and you didn't
want to believe they were capable
of that kind of betrayal.

But naïvety doesn't protect you
—it just delays pain.

Everything terrible will catch up.

The new me is:

terrifying in her awareness,
grateful for her resilience,
comfortable being alone.

FOR ME!
THE GODDESS:
UNLEASH HER AND NEVER FORGET HER

I have burned enough bridges
to learn that a man who wants you
will do everything in his power
to have you (and a man who *doesn't*,
will let you know in his own way).

I have learned to want myself
when no one else does.

What a healing experience:
to recognize that I was
worth loving all along.

I am not above anyone.
I am not better than my past,
but I am different.

And if you fail to see how a girl
that once begged for love
is now full of it:

you are still nostalgic for the old me.

EULOGY

I don't want to write your eulogy.
I'll probably see you in a month or two,
throwing cuss words instead
of rocks at my window,
butting your cigarettes
in the flowers.

OCEAN

1

The world gives women "guilt"
to package it nicely because it knows
we can make anything beautiful.

Men just leave that shit everywhere.

A man once refused to pull out,
put his guilt directly inside me.

Wondered why I
became so distressed
now that the illusion
that I was safe had broken.

2

My body is not a fossil of every man
who has ever touched me.

It is a living,
breathing,
ocean.

I once read that every cell
in our body dies and replaces itself
in seven years time.

I wonder how many new versions of me
would walk right past you.

HEAVEN

I wonder why God
didn't give women
chameleon skin
so if a man ever grabbed us
we could disappear into
the backdrop:

invisible.
untouchable.
safe.

I wonder why he gave us skin
like silk and lips
like clouds
and bodies
like valleys.

Why did God
make us heaven
and leave the gates open?

LIKE RAPUNZEL

Anytime a man has crossed my boundaries,
it has been met with the words:

"Sorry, I just couldn't control myself."

The number of times I have brushed
this truth off my skin terrifies me.

Beauty is an aphrodisiac—but
it shouldn't come at the
price of trauma.

It's too steep.

I would hide myself away for years
if I could unmeet the men of my past.

Like Rapunzel—but I
never let my hair down.

Safety is the only thing
that feels like home
and I keep searching for it:

in arms that hold me
but don't ask for anything,

in men who love me before
they see me with my clothes off.

ME TOO

Me too, she says

because her body has only ever
loosely belonged to her.
For years, it has been at someone else's
disposal, at someone else's mercy.

Me too, she says

because consent is still a blurred line
for people who choose to colour outside of it.
Her skin a track record of strangers' touches.

Me too, she says

because no measurable force could stop the men
who've been taught in good conscience:
that a woman's body is not her own,
that it belongs to *everyone.*

CATCALL

Whistles carry the weight
of oppression but you
continue your routine
feigning ignorance.

—no wonder you only speak
to women from a distance

BODY COUNT

Ask me how many men I've slept with
and I'll ask you to do the math.

Do I count the guy who slipped in
without a condom
while we kissed in his car,
because he didn't feel like ruining
the moment by asking?

Or the one who hit my face
halfway through, like it's
something we discussed?

What about the man who said
he fucked me in the shower,
but I don't remember
a single thing but
my own foot stepping in.

Do you count when
I didn't consent,
because I don't.

But men won't do the math.
Men won't do the math.

1.
2.
3.
4.
5.
6.
7.

1.
2.
3.
4.
5.
6.
7.

1.
2.
3.
4.
5.
6.
7.

1.
2.
3.
4.
5.
6.
7.

A COMPACT THING

You reach for my body
the way roses bloom
on a time-lapse.

Slowly—
and then,
all at once.

The bartender pulls me aside,
wiping condensation and worry
on her tiny embroidered apron

while men watch like it's
the Discovery Channel,
their own desire collecting
dust for too long.

You lift me onto the edge
of the pool table—playfully,
hands cupped around my arms
like I am a watermelon
you are testing at the grocery store.

Knocking on my surface
like you believe,

the best women are hollow too.

I am a thing on display,

a testament to how men
use other men as outlets:
they live vicariously through
their advances.

Desire is never a compact thing;
it is a complex thing.

—you make a show of my consent
when I haven't given it

STREETCAR

I pull my skirt down when I leave the house
because if I don't, my uncle will tell
my mother what I am wearing.

He will call her at work and grossly exaggerate.

If I was his own daughter,
he wouldn't let me leave the house.

There's no use explaining how I just
want to feel the sun on my bare skin
when I'm sitting on the streetcar.

TEACH HER BOTH

To the men who taught me early on
that having a body like mine is a burden,

I hope you find self-control.

To the father who taught me by example
that being present in a child's life is optional,

I hope you find better judgement.

To the mother who taught me only one side
of the story, that a girl's safety is far more
important than her freedom,

I wish you taught me both.

BODY

1

My best friend thinks showing your body is a sin.
She tells me I'm a threat to her salvation.

She doesn't sound like herself,
like she's ad-libbing the words
of her brother's devout wife
who used to shame her
for wearing crop tops.

She unfollows me on Instagram.

I didn't get the chance to ask her if she
thinks every girl with an OnlyFans
won't get into heaven.

2

My mother believes women above a size 8
shouldn't publicly celebrate their bodies.

She jeers at them for wearing bikinis or miniskirts
and having attractive, muscular boyfriends.

For being happy in their skin like it's taboo.

She comments on my flat chest, my fat ass,
pulls at the waistband of everything I own
just like she did when I was growing up.

Testing how tight my clothes are.
If I can breathe in them.
Policing my body.

But my body is not something to be
supervised. Questioned. Measured.

If I shaved my pussy,
I was scolded for "promiscuity."
If I didn't shave my legs,
I was scolded for being unkempt.

Every time I left the house became an argument on modesty. My clothes seemed to infer things that I wasn't aware of.

But my grandmother always sided with my choice of fashion over comfort. For wearing something that made me feel like myself despite my mother's grievances.

3

Women learn how to love themselves
from other women.

Maybe that's why I'm so confused.

Maybe that's why I used to wrap a towel
around myself in the change room of the public pool
like I was practicing bondage with terry cloth.

Like my skin held every shame that was projected
onto me since birth and exposing it would
show other women the same truth.

That even our nakedness does not belong to us.

That others still have the liberty to make laws
on our bodies and how we use them
and how we honour them.

But I refuse to teach my future daughter
the same toxic modesty that was taught to me.

I refuse to pass down the idea that our bodies are
inheritors of shame simply because we are women.

4

Women learn how to love themselves
from how men love them.

My first boyfriend asked me
if I would ever get my breasts "done."

I was 15 years old but confident that
I wouldn't develop anymore because
the women in my family are petite.

His question wrapped itself around me
like a rope without an end point.
It sat on my chest like a brick
—*deflating* me.

I wish I had argued that the physics
of my body were not his to decide.

But I could not unlearn the knowledge that
I was somehow defective in his eyes,
and every time he touched me after that
felt like the wrong kind of apology.

5

Women learn how to love themselves
from every source except the one
we have within ourselves.

Our intuition. Our ability
to manifest something better
than what the past has taught us.

I am honouring my skin
for the home it has always been.

But I am cutting away the rotten wires,
the floorboards that lift when you step on them
—evidence of the men who put all
their weight on me:

their baggage,
their fear of love,
their insecurities with the hope
that I would transform them.

Men who considered my body
the morse code to morals,
who mistook my kindness
for submission because it
suited them better.

6

Resilience comes when you are forced
to gut the past like an old house.
Dismantle and start over while
keeping its lessons close in hand.

My best friend chose to surrender
her autonomy and condemn mine.

I forgive her for thinking that women
should ever compromise the freedom
that belongs to us.

My mother taught me that modesty is
the only acceptable way for a woman to live
because she thought it would keep me safe.

I sympathize with her fears
because all women have them.

I reframe the comments of men who believed
I was flawed in a way that could not be fixed.

I am worth more than their hands
could ever promise.

ABSENCE

They say we look for our parents
in every relationship.
We do it subconsciously.
We won't even notice.

Maybe that's why
I keep looking for my father
and finding his *absence*

in men who collectively think
I'm beautiful but refuse to make roots.

Men who take every precaution
when they are trying to love me
so it feels insincere.

Men who hide their bad parts:

the women who left them
the past that shaped them

in case I might share the
same urge to run.

But I refuse to love or be loved
from a place of self-protection.

I can't make roots with men who
withhold intimacy because they feel
safer just to watch me be vulnerable.

I won't make space for something
that comes with an expiration date
but promises it doesn't.

WHOLE

I want to forget about you.

The way young girls
use flowers
to predict if love is true,
to beg nature for it to last.

I want to gather
all the broken petals
and lay them around myself,
like I am a planet and they are
the moons in my orbit.

Whether you stay
or whether you go,

I have always been whole.

LEAVING ME SIGNS

1

I spent years preoccupied with people
who couldn't love me because

they assumed that love was something
that fell into their lap and tended for itself.

They didn't believe in sanding yourself down
until only the truth was left.

I used the potential for love to both comfort and
blindside me and when real love came to face me:

I hid from its embrace.
I prayed I was unrecognizable.

I was terrified that love would ask questions
I didn't want to answer.

Love would hold me accountable:

the times I surrendered to men,
simply because I ran out of ways to say "no."

Love would tell me I didn't look
in the right places for it.

Love would say it left signs that I walked past.

Love would laugh at my expense.

I would try to explain to love
that I never made roots
because it never felt
how they promised it would

and every man I asked to love me
brought me to a new low point
because I didn't love myself first.

2

I don't want love to be an extension
of every trauma I've ever had.
I don't want it to feel sour in my stomach
or make me feel like I am losing
myself in the process.

I want love that tells me what I already know:

that I am worthy of it,
that it will never stop leaving me signs
—praying I notice.

Thank you
LUCKY NUMBER: 222
"YOU WILL BE BLESSED WITH A LOVE THAT STOPS TIME"

GRIEVE THE PAST

Grieve the past so it doesn't
trail you with crumbs
asking you to come back.

The irony in how old habits
beg us to notice them
once we've outgrown them.

Going backwards is like an
act of penance that never
leaves anyone fulfilled.

Sometimes,
I want history to repeat itself.
I imagine I could abandon to it
—*freer* this time because
I exist in the future.

I can predict the pain:
prepare myself for every curveball,
every gut-wrenching loss.

I imagine I would be kinder to myself
and draw a line in the sand this time

using curated wisdom that only comes
from knowing the outcome
because it has already happened.

Almost like a sickly dream from
sleeping on an empty stomach
and waking up craving the touch
of all your former lovers.

The only thing you really want
is the agency you never had.

Grieve the past but why put
yourself through it *twice?*

CURSE

I will never use men
to heal again.

My body is not a token
of my self-worth.

A man's touch, no matter
how sweet, is its own
sort of curse.

SLEEPING BEAUTY
CONSCIOUS Sex

DIGGING UP GRAVES

Once upon a time,
I used men to feel alive.

So perhaps, I wasn't that bothered
when they used me too.

Fragility attracts the worst kind
of people, but when we feel numb
any feeling is worth having.

I was playing emotional blackmail
with myself and I couldn't stop.

SELF
INFLICTED

When a woman puts a man's needs
before her own, it is because
she is desperate to be loved

and the true test of whether
you are using sex for connection
or approval is how empty
you feel afterwards.

I cannot go back in time
and sometimes just writing
about the past
is like digging up graves
I haven't walked by in years.

But I have learned that the
only way to heal is to make
the commitment to live
consciously every day of my life.

Past habits may comfort us
in their blatant familiarity
but they should only
serve as a warning.

Pay attention to why you crave
validation from empty people.
They cannot even give it to themselves.

Are you falling in love?
Do you like sex that much or
are you looking for a distraction?

These are questions
I have learned to ask myself
because I can't always trust how I feel
because it's manic or hyperbolic
and I don't know
how to see things clearly.

All of my life I have worn
rose-coloured glasses.

Paying attention is painful.
Noticing things instead
of brushing them under the rug
requires an excess of courage
I never had before.

But I want to see everything
I tried to hide myself from
so I can grieve and finally,

let it go.

being hurt / being loved

How is it that being loved brings up all the hurt?

OLD PAIN

I call the guy
I lost my virginity to
8 years later

—*fresh* with old pain.

I tell him about my
new neighbourhood.

How the trees seem bigger.
How it's close to the city but quiet.
How the lock on my bedroom door
is broken from use.

We laugh like old friends
who didn't part ways
on my driveway between
tears and a confession.

He says without saying it:

I feel nothing for you

and I think of how many years
I let the darkness of his absence
sit in my heart,
take up space,
keep me company.

I think of how many
years I missed someone
who let me go
so easily,
like he had practiced it.

I ASKED GOD

1

I asked God to fix
the gap in my teeth
in Grade 5 because
school pictures
were coming up.
Two years later,
it fixed by itself
and the dentist
who tried to sell
my single mom
on the idea of braces
thought it was a rare
kind of luck.

2

I asked God to bring
my first love back
from whatever grass
he thought was greener
because his absence
felt like the
wrong ending.
I would regret
asking God for this
because a boy who
breaks your heart once,
considers it
a revolving door.

CLOSED DOORS

I am weak for men
who can stand without me.

I imagine they harvest
their confidence by hand:
water it at night from the
rain that collects in gutters.
Steal sunshine from
underneath our noses.

I think about this when they
hold the small of my back
like they are taping
a broken glass together
or kiss my mouth like they are
sucking out my potential.

I want to think like a man,
mimic that dangerous fearlessness,
that self-induced ignorance
and belief that "I am God."

But instead, I remember I am me.

—women operate like life is full of closed doors
and only men have the keys to them

GOOD MEN

1

Good men love me but I rarely let them.
I make them climb fences called *friendship,*
make them jump through hoops just to hold me
platonically—stunted by my own
fear of being loved in a way
that doesn't unsettle me.

Good men love me but I pretend my past
is a purse full of crumpled up
fortune cookie slips.

I act like I had no control over it.

One fortune reads,

"The thrill of the chase
will leave you exhausted"

but I can't replace that excitement.

Hope is the most spontaneous
thing in the world because
no one can tell you
not to have it.

2

I convince myself
through trial and error
with ill-suited men,
that I will outgrow affection
that doesn't need to be
constantly earned.

Watered. Waited on.

3

Good men love me and
they foreshadow the fact
that I could let their love
rewrite my whole history
—let it change the way
I go searching for grief
like it's something
I lost and want back.

Good men love me
and they are convincing
in their sincerity
but I still cling to
the belief that men
will hurt me before they ever
honour me because that's
what life has taught me.

4

And whether it's
a self-fulfilling prophecy
or just fate dealing me a
hand of cards I can't seem
to shake—either way,
I am vulnerable.

And whomever I give a chance
to see my scars up close,
to make their own assumptions:
they'll have the power to call
their *bluff* on my hope,
to disappoint me
in every way I know.

—to the men who left the minute I became accustomed to them;

this one's for you

THE CONTRAST

1

The contrast between men who love me
and men who don't is painfully obvious.

Each one leaves clues
but there is nothing to solve.
The truth is visible in plain sight.

To one, I am desire: easy and tangible.
Nothing to analyze past my skin, my mouth.

I am a memory to tuck away during a dry spell.
An earring or a hair tie left behind
in passion's haste.

A good dream you want to relive by heart

—but it
slips
away,
always.

To the other, I am something real:
equal parts caution and thrill.

We kiss like we are exchanging stars
between our mouths.

We make wishes no one will ever hear.
The kind reserved for diaries with locks
and time capsules.

They recognize the wounds from
losing yourself and gathering
only the parts worth keeping.

2

I never choose men who nurture me.
I never choose men who share their strength,
who convince me against my own flaws.

I choose men who teach me things
I would be better off not knowing.
I choose men who show me with their lack
of empathy that I am alone in this world.

3

Nothing about you scares me because
nothing about you feels familiar.

I am guilty of surrendering my power
but you don't want to take it.

You protect me in the ways
I haven't learned how.

I know that I can trust you because
I don't have to convince myself I am safe.

—and what a new feeling that is

IN YOURS

You are a dream I had
that transformed into a person.

Your self-esteem does not change
like the weather.

Your childhood trauma does not
follow you everywhere you go
like a sad reminder.

There is no list of your faults
floating in my head,
simply because I can't find any.

You have no skeletons to brush under the rug.
You give me no reason to hold my temper.

You're the clean slate I'll never be
but get to share a bed with.

But I want to know
how you got to this place
of feeling safe in your own skin.

I am not there yet.

I am still trying to make a home in *yours.*

TRACING PAPER

You trace my body with your
hands / tongue / fingers / mouth.

I am nothing like;
I am exactly what you imagined.

The paradox of someone new.

TWO MONTHS

It takes my boyfriend
two months to make me *come*

—the female orgasm
relying on an elusive,
ever-changing formula.

My body is beautiful
but closed off,
an intimacy roadblock

but when he touches me
I don't have the urge

to push him away or
reclaim space for myself.

I let him kiss the parts
others neglected,

let him unearth my
most complex desires

and when I *do* come,
I cry out like I've been gutted.

All the times I never came
in the hands of men

who never learned how to
cherish a woman,

flood out of me.

Sex can be wonderful
and healing.

It can change the way
you feel about yourself.

When used the right way
it is an outlet for growth,

an expression of love.

Everything with him
feels brand new.

I rediscover my body and
everything it is capable of.

We play like children who
practice kissing under
the dining room table;

we have no rules.

The body I once tortured
transforms into a temple:

a place of rest and worship,
a limitless source of joy.

I feel safe for the
first time in years

and it's not because
I am craving escape.

It is not the untrustworthy
thrill I am used to.

I do not sacrifice anything
out of obligation or fear.

I do not bend myself into
something worth desiring.

I am in love and it's terrifying
to be so exposed,

to work backwards with you and
tell you that I don't have many

happy memories with the people
I shared myself with before.

I only have a few I save
for nights when loneliness
curates false endings.

And you promise me
we will make more:

like my bank of happiness
is your concern too,

like my healing
is your priority.

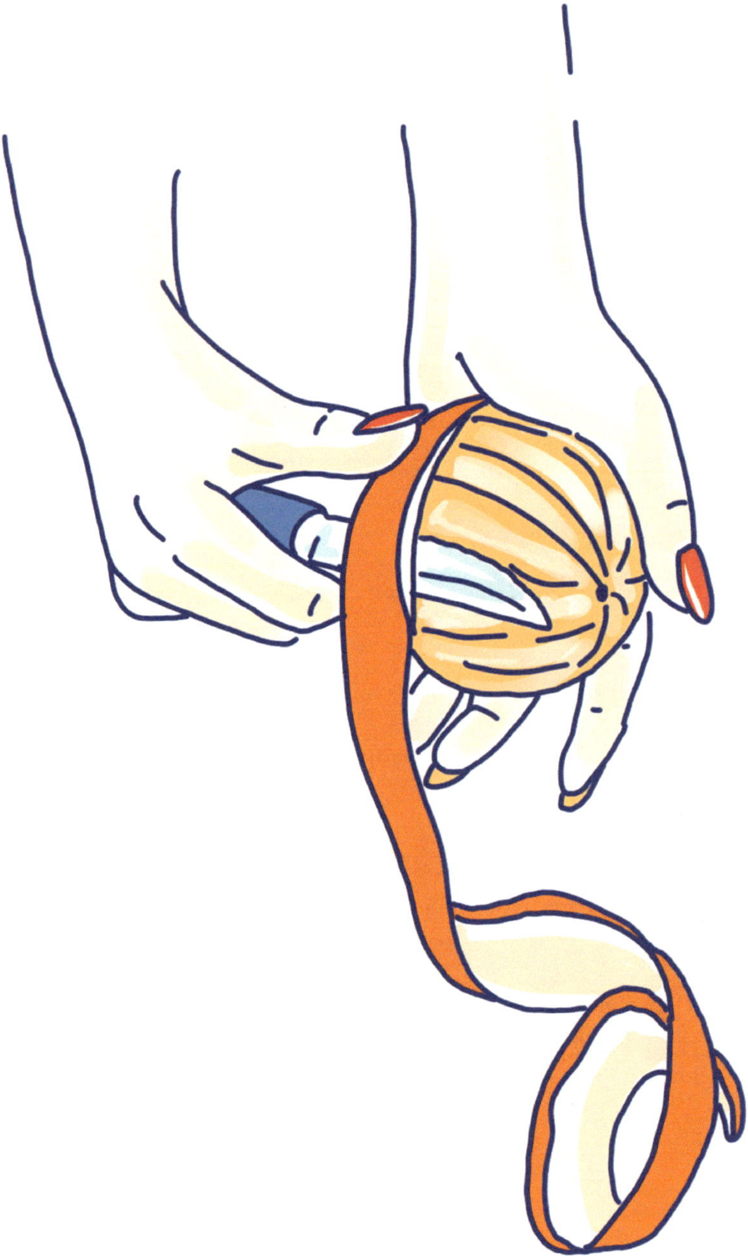

MAGIC

You touch me
as though peeling off
my past with your fingers.

You have this magic.

I've never felt quite this safe,
exactly this loved before.

Losing you would
mean something.
You're not a heartache
I could sleep on.

You are a person I would mourn.

THE LOVE

You wrap me in the love I've wanted for years.

GOOD THINGS

1

I only want to feel
good things when I'm with you.

Maybe this is a stretch.
Maybe this is asking too much.
Maybe God will laugh.

But you're gentle with me
and I could get used to the
butterflies in my stomach
without the predictable feeling
of something going wrong.

2

It's a miracle how we can
both *come* at the same time.

We are full of complexes
and unresolved pain
and the fatigue
that comes from constantly
evolving and not being able
to decide which versions
of ourselves we like best.

3

And sometimes, when we argue
I think you're ready to leave
because you see my trauma
for the clever chameleon it is:

the way it reveals itself
in convincing layers and
makes me someone else entirely.

I struggle to show you my past
in a way that doesn't feel
like I'm reliving it.

—how do I tell you my truth
without making you a witness?

BACK TO ME

How do I come back to me?

I want someone to give me an easy answer,
one that doesn't involve uprooting
old pain just to hold it.

Wounds are like roots that get tangled
around our whole body and we forget
how we lived before that suffering.

We tell ourselves: *it will always be like this.*

But I can't keep looking behind me.
There is nothing left for me there,
only quiet and compromise and fear.

I act like I'm lost but
I was never found to begin with.
The beauty in that
is that I really *do* have
my whole life ahead of me.

And the longer I love myself,
the more I am convinced
I will get the life I want.
It doesn't feel so far away anymore.
It doesn't feel like it belongs to someone else.

SEASONS

I am confident
I won't leave you:
a secret I don't say out loud
because my track record with men
would give you anxiety
because there is something
so impossible about
having to choose one person
for all the seasons of your life.

—how can I truly know what I want
if I'm still changing?

love
all
of you

ANGLES

You
convince me
that beauty is
not what we're taught.
Beg me to notice myself:
the angles I hate,
the face I worry
I may never
grow to
love.

OUT OF REACH

You have waited for the right woman
for a long time—the slew of dates
which ended as unceremoniously
as they began.

The girls who left
their drugstore eyelashes
in your bathroom sink
like a sullen reminder.

Something about me
stirs something in you
that has been neglected for so long.

The belief that you
really *do* deserve love,
that it is not so out of reach.

HOMME

THE WRONG PERSON

I grieve things that have already passed me.

I remember the joys
of the wrong person:
the newness, the freedom,
the experiences of love.

Sometimes, I try to recreate the past
so that the future seems less scary:

like the comfort of
an old blanket
or a stuffed bear
when everything seems uncertain.

Men who I have already been with
don't frighten me.
They have already seen
the worst parts of me.

You can always count on someone
who historically loves you,
who has passed every test.

And after many years,
still answers the phone like you are
his favourite person coming back to him.

WHOLE LIVES

I have lived whole lives
without you.

I have squeezed out
the venom that says:

something is missing.

I have sat in the sun
telling stories until my
ocean hair dried
into the untamed curls
you used to fall asleep on.

But when you come back
with dirt on your knees
and new bruises,
you have my heart again
like it never left you.

LOST TIME

I lament lost time but never
lost lovers because even the memory
of passion serves a purpose.

I keep the touch of every man
who has come close to me
in my mind for safekeeping.

Sometimes we need the reminder
that desire is an ocean wave
capable of taking everything.

THE SCOPE OF DESIRE

I don't need to define myself
through the scope of desire.
But the body remembers pleasure,
the body remembers.

I cannot live without pleasure
that stops me in the middle of the day
and asks me for a moment of
reverence, appreciation, quiet.

My unfulfilled fantasies call out to me
louder with each passing day.

It's like trying to stifle my own moans.
It's like keeping my heart locked in a cage.

My fantasies show up
in dreams that feel so real,
I am disoriented upon waking.

I want to stay asleep until
pleasure is inscribed
on every inch of my body.

Because pleasure is truly
the greatest high,
the most transformative gift
(after love, that is).

Because the body
remembers pleasure,
the body remembers.

SOMEONE ELSE

You attract more bees
with honey than vinegar
but there is nothing sweet
left to say,
no more touches
between pillowcases
when we've chosen sleep
but still want to tease each other.

I vowed to not become sour
if things didn't work out
but it's a harder promise
to live up to:
when love is not
on your side,
when it has already found
someone else.

SHE'S MY HONEY
HE'S MY HONEY

SURVEILLANCE

1

I'm not sure why "love" in my life
always feels like surveillance.

A man who loves me
becomes a second shadow.

I only have a few hours of solitude
and even in those, I ruminate on how
he will perceive my actions in his absence,
in the layers of any innocent thing I do.

I moderate my behaviour and I can't tell if it's
to prevent an argument or quiet a deeper issue.

Everything I do is open to interpretation,
leaving me in a battleground of my own making.

1:31
what are you wearing to class?
1:32
...hopefully nothing slutty...
1:47
Answer your phone!!!

2

I am learning that it is necessary to separate myself
from people I love in healthy ways.

Boundaries—a silver lining unbeknownst to me,
make me feel the safest I have ever felt.

I trace this back to my roots when my grandfather
used to tell me with complete certainty,

"In life, always keep something for yourself."

I struggled to understand what he meant
at the time because in my eyes:
if I loved someone,
if I *truly* loved them,
I would give them everything I had.

There would be no doubt.

3

The error in this grand belief is that love
(like all meaningful parts of life)
is fluid, ever-changing, and evolving.
It requires both give and take,
both surrender and protection.

I am accepting that I can *love* and still
keep parts of myself for me.
I can love and still share what I choose.
My whole life story does not belong
to who I share a bed with.
Love does not have to leave me
completely bare to be authentic.

Giving love in any capacity is
already a vulnerable act.
We don't know how our love
will be received or if it
will be reciprocated,
but we give it freely.

4

A woman who can read soul ties
and uncover past lives reveals to me
three things I need in my relationships.

Safety.
Privacy.
Freedom.

She speaks about a lack of these elements
when I was growing up and I pause in disbelief
because I feel so genuinely
seen and heard by a stranger.

Instant connection has a way of humbling us
and reminding us of our humanity.

Healers exist and they want to bring us
back to ourselves if we are willing.

But it's not easy.

Most people resist the truth
with every fibre of their being.
The tapestry of their life stays hidden for years.

Better to remain safely hidden than truly seen.

5

I wonder sometimes if any love exists
without some degree of ownership,
without that lingering trace
of surveillance.

Because I have never had *this* kind of love,
it's like a forbidden fruit in my mind
where I can be:

Seen, but not watched.
Heard, but not followed.
Loved, but not *had.*

HOW CAN I BE YOURS
WITHOUT LOSING MYSELF ?

FORGOT

I forgot what desire was:
that pulse in my pussy,
that feeling of running a red light.

I am starving for something
I have felt a million times
in my solitude.

It seems to disappear
when I am partnered
and in love.

It's like the kindness drowns it,
the familiarity asks me
to forget it altogether.

That is my sacrifice:
my own desire,
obsolete.

I need to feel something dangerous.
I need to be reminded
I am *that* woman.

The one I love so much.

Who never denies her body
what it wants the most.
Who never quiets her own desire.

ONLY IN DESIRE

For years, I spoke only in desire:

knotted hair I neglected to brush,
summer dresses with the straps too loose,
lipstick the shade of red wax that seals letters.

I was giddy in my lack of inhibitions.
Overdressed in my hope for an adventure.
Girls gone wild but in the daylight.

Men responded well to this:
my eager spirit like a ribbon
on their wrists,
keeping them hostage
while setting them free.

The convenience of fantasy is that it
promises more and comforts you
better than the truth.

The men I entertained
left my arms more inspired
then they came—and I too
was inspired.

Desire is an easy high.
It costs you nothing.
It tastes the way sunlight
would taste if you could
coat your entire mouth in it.

"He wants me even when I don't
want myself" is the strangest relief.
It's like coming home after a long day
and running a bath with your clothes on.

You can still feel the warm water touching
your skin but it's been poisoned with
your deepest truth.

The men you've shown your body to
haven't really seen you.
They've seen a projection.

Insecurity disguised as agency.
Pain disguised as euphoria.

Lost girls are like tokens for them
and I fulfilled the stereotype
of every lost girl.

I waited for the familiar glow
on my phone screen.

As though there was something
innately satisfying
about my self-sabotage
or the tangled roots of my
self-diagnosed nymphomania.

I came to understand
that men loved the idea
that they were wearing me thin,
exposing me,
capitalizing on my pain.

Men who soul-search
in a woman's broken lust
are like a broken record.
You can expect the same
thing from each one.

Nothing.

Now, I am learning
how to speak in love.

The men who used to move mountains
just to touch me have become rigid—
as if they owe me an explanation
for the desire they once
couldn't keep quiet.

Their desire cannot exist
the way it did before because
I am unwilling to receive it.
It is too empty for me.

My body is now an extension
of my heart: resilient.

Impossible to walk away from.

THE RIGHT QUESTIONS

Maybe I am the silver lining
you've been searching for:
the soft landing,
some version of home

and maybe to me,
you are just an illusion:
preparation for the real thing
but convincingly close to it.

When you kiss me I tell you,
"It's about time."

I tell this to the crook
of your shoulder
because I'm not ready
to look into your eyes
because you will see

that I have been waiting
my whole life
for the type of love
I don't have to question
or convince myself I want.

We chase the things we worry
we won't get to have with
the utmost conviction.

I act like you are an answer
but I'm still figuring out
the right questions
to ask myself.

TAROT

HOW DO I?

How do I honour myself
after years of self-betrayal?

How do I trust myself
after bad outcomes?

How do I love myself when
there are so many parts
that need to be healed?

—with the compassion,
patience and grace
I give so easily to others

WOMAN OF MY DREAMS

1

I am the woman of my dreams
but for years I believed that I wasn't.
For years I told myself—"just wait."

Love will come and convince you
of what you should already know.

Love will do its beautiful job and all
you will have to do is receive it.

Except receiving love for someone
who has spent most of their life
receiving the opposite
feels like receiving a gift
that I wasn't expecting
(so I show up empty-handed).

Receiving love feels like getting
a full night's rest and then being
overtaken by anxiety when
my feet leave my warm bed.

My mind begins to spiral with
a million different scenarios.

Questions like:

Will this love last?
Is this "the one"?
Why do I feel so undecided?

How can I trust my intuition
if I have been programmed
through years of abuse
to always feel like I need
to protect myself?

How can I receive love
without receiving fear?

2

Navigating love is scary for those
who know that receiving love
has always come at a great expense.

Receiving love has always included loss.

All of my lovers seem to possess me.
They shift me from my place in the
driver's seat of my own life.

My lovers hold all the cards
and I desire the whole deck.
I need to feel its weight in my hands
—evidence that it's still mine
and it always was.

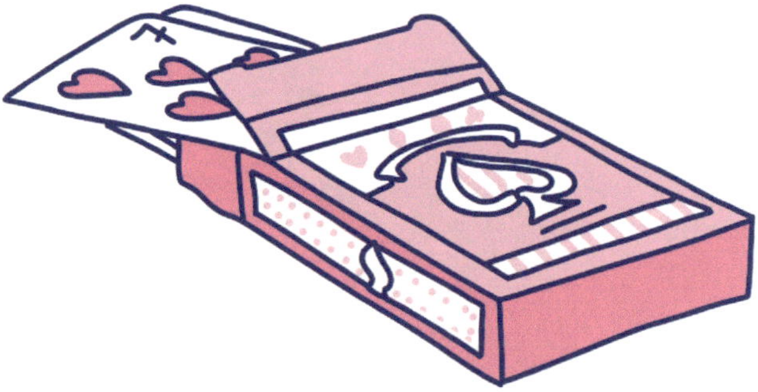

3

If I want to enjoy life,
if I really want to *live*—

I have to be okay with uncertainty.

Because no matter how many
promises I make with
different men,
I always end up
in the same place.

No matter how loved I am,
it never feels like enough.

4

I'm learning that the love of my life
should always be me.

And if I can't hold myself
in my own arms and believe
that things will be okay:

No one's love will make me feel safe.
No one's love will feel "just right."
No one's love will be enough.

Dream
Girl

THE RIGHT PERSON

1

The right person will tell you:
"you are safe here."
They will take your pain
and neatly package it so
it doesn't scare you anymore.

The right person will convince you
that the joys in life
override the doubts,
that every version of you
existed for a reason
but now you can be
who you truly are.

The right person will set you free.

2

And sometimes,
it's hard to tell who
to trust with that job
because fate tells you
that what's meant for you
won't pass you
but fear tells you
that a love like that:

a love so beautiful and rare
it opens you right up

is not something
everyone gets to have.

3

I have let go of men
who loved me with their
entire soul because I didn't
feel true peace in their arms.

I didn't feel the ease
or the type of calm that
I expect to feel with a man
who can hold me for hours
and not expect a single word.

I want a love like that so badly
but it always seems to pass me.

4

And maybe I'm not ready
to give my life to someone
who has already lived theirs.
Maybe there are questions
only I can answer for myself.

But I want to get to that place
where I let love in,
where I trust it
to do its job.

epilogue

girls (really do) grow up

GIRLS GROW UP

Girls grow up,
dizzy in their innocence
and fall into boys' beds with the idea
that they will find solace there.

Girls grow up
looking for proof
they are worth loving
through the measure of desire
when their beauty is recognized
as something to explore
behind closed doors.

Girls grow up
and pay ironic homage
to the mirror that was
wrong all these years:

they *are* beautiful.

A boy's revelations have changed
the way she'll carry herself
in the hallways of other girls
who share lip gloss
before giving blow jobs
like it's a ritual.

Intimacy for the first time
is being held in a bed the same
size as your own (and hoping his
parents don't come home early
enough to assume you are just
another "unhinged" girl)
so you can daydream on his chest
that's been caved in since birth.

So you can try on all his clothes:
rugby jersey with the number 11,
baggy jeans your family would
tease him relentlessly about
if you ever brought him to dinner and
the tacky belt buckles that remind you
of car emblems people used to steal
and keep on a shelf in their bedroom
as trophies of misdemeanor.

One of those things that can
only be fun if you're never caught.

Boys grow up
making paper chains
with the pieces of girls' hearts
they are gifted in high school
and tie them to their bed frames
as proof—that girls will do
anything in their pursuit
to be seen and loved in a way
that comforts them.

Boys grow up
making promises
that sound like metaphors
they can't remember and
writing internet poems
in yearbooks:

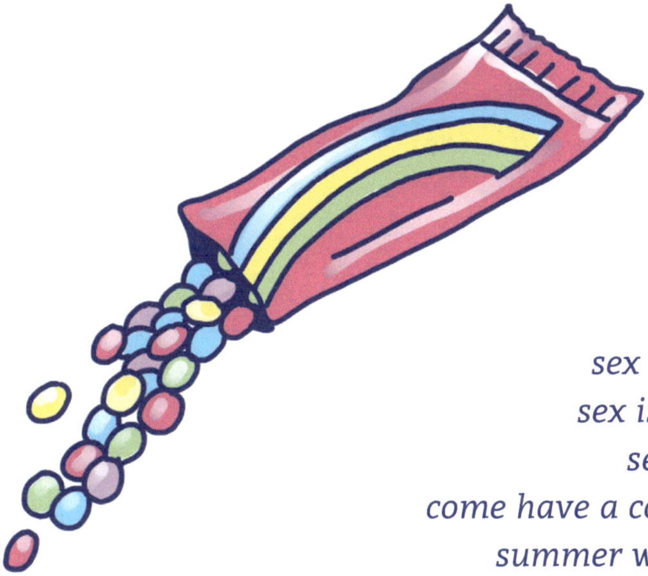

sex is green.
sex is yellow.
sex is red.
come have a colourful
*summer with me.**

**an actual entry in my mother's*
high school yearbook

Boys grow up
following girls they only
half-like to their lockers
with the inside doors
covered with polaroids:

close-ups of
their belly rings
and drunk photos
with their girlfriends
who look like clones
of the same insecurities

because boys know
that carrying books
is the foreplay to first base
and hitting *any* base means
they can tell the whole school
they took your virginity
without question.

Girls grow up
but we never stop looking
for ways to betray ourselves.
First, in the revelation that
our first love *wasn't* love.
He just convinced us
long enough to get
what he wanted:

a paper chain so perfect,
he could fold it in two
without it breaking.

about the author

Christie Maragos is
a poet and spoken word artist
who likes to call herself the
Elle Woods of poetry.

You can find her performing
at events across Toronto.

Girls Grow Up is
her 10-year vision come to life.

Connect with her love of pink,
pretty dresses and poetry
on Instagram @christiemaragos
and online at christiemaragos.com

about the artist

Julia Monson is
a Toronto-based illustrator
known for her quirky
and dreamlike paintings.

Connect with her
cheeky and romantic art
on Instagram @julesmonson
and online at juliamonsonshop.com

poetic works
by christie maragos

petite girl precious heart

angels in heaven

crybaby

never stop
writing

never stop
dreaming

never lose
hope

First Printing, 2025.

This is a work of nonfiction.

Creative direction and poetry by: Christie Maragos
Cover art and illustrations by: Julia Monson

Author photo: Christie Maragos, 2024
Pink background: Pinterest (source unknown)

christiemaragos.com

ISBN 978-1-0690067-0-7

Manufactured by Amazon.ca
Bolton, ON

43610070R00129